STOP HIDING BEHIND YOURSELF

7 Principles to Exposing
the Hidden You
and
Discovering Your
SPARKLE Effect

TAWAWN LOWE

Printed in the United States of America

Tawawn Lowe

STOP HIDING BEHID YOURSELF

7-Principles to Exposing the Hidden You and Discovering Your SPARKLE Effect / by Tawawn Lowe

978 – 0 – 978809 0– 2 – 7

DISCLAIMER

The purpose of this book is to educate and entertain. The author or publisher does not guarantee that anyone following the techniques, suggestions, tips, ideas, or strategies will become successful. The author and publisher shall have neither liability or responsibility to anyone with respect to any loss or damage caused, or alleged to be caused, directly or indirectly by the information contained in this book.

Get FREE bonus on How to Confront Your Fear

www.TAWAWNLOWE.com

Acknowledgements

I'm thankful and grateful for the opportunity to work and walk in my purpose helping women to create lives that allow them to walk in their own shoes. I embrace my assignment, and all the women who have entrusted me to help make a difference in their lives.

This book is dedicated to all those who have ever found themselves STUCK at a crossroads, only to realize that the only thing standing between them and creating the life their desire is themselves.

This dedication also goes out to all my family and friends who have supported me on this journey to assist women with walking in their own shoes. Thank you for your unconditional support and encouragement. I pray that God will return back to you the encouragement, love and support 100-fold.

To my mother Charlotte Harrison who I am eternally grateful for supported all my endeavors and believed in my ability when I didn't believe in myself.

To everyone who has helped get this book from my brain to your hands. Special thanks to Lisa Handon, Melisa Jenkins, and Kimberly Brooks for pushing me and stretching me to another level to make my work and this project a success.

To God, for giving me these gifts and talents to help women to get UNSTUCK, navigate through life transitions, to make their life their business; and get to the business of their life.

STOP HIDING BEHIND YOURSELF

7-Principles to Exposing Your Hidden Self and Discovering

Your *SPARKLE* effect

By Tawawn Lowe

To:

_____

From:

_____

What Makes A Person SHINE?
Being willing to take the journey
within to find out who you really are,
and letting what's hiding in the
shadows come forth and SHINE!

For additional information on Tawawn
Lowe, please visit her on the web at
www.TAWAWNLOWE.com
or email her at
INFO@TAWAWNLOWE.com

Tawawn would like to hear from you!

Go to **www.TawawnLowe.com/testimonials** and leave her a
few comments about how this book has helped you.

Table of Contents

Introduction

What is keeping you from being your best self and living the life you deserve? Why are you afraid to let your inner light shine? It's time to bring your hidden power and potential out of the shadows and into the light. You are like a diamond, created to sparkle and shine, even with your imperfections. What more proof do you need to validate that you too are a precious gem?

I know this sounds like a cliché, but you only have one life to live, and that gift of life is far too precious to waste. Life is choice driven, and every day you are faced with the choice of how, or if, you will take full advantage of this gift that has been given to you. You have the choice to live in the NOW, fully present and engaged, taking forward action to become your ultimate best while giving your best and receiving the best that life has to offer. Or you can choose to let the toxins of your life's experiences keep you shrinking inward, scared to let the dimmer switch of your life rise to your full wattage potential.

The only barrier standing between you and confronting your hidden self is you. This is your time to embrace the opportunity to look inward and shine a light where excuses, limiting beliefs, fear and self-defeating attitudes (darkness) reside. By releasing and replacing those things that block your light from shining, you can more fully reach your potential.

You are amazing, wonderful, and fearfully created in God's image. When God created you He broke the mold. He made you a one-of-a-kind being, giving you a unique journey full of experiences to prepare you for your purpose. You are a brilliant gem with unique gifts and talents that need to be shared with the world.

You are worthy and deserve to let your sparkle effect show. It is your responsibility to take the journey to rediscovering who you are, so you can know what you really want and create a life that is neither behind your shadow, or a mask.

The beauty of this gift of life is your journey. It is full of opportunities to create the life that allows you to be your authentic self, living life with purpose, and owning your own success. It also provides second chances when you don't get it right the first, second, or third time.

Getting out of your own way to discover your sparkle effect is a major goal. As with any goal there will be obstacles. The journey won't be easy and change is hard. Be patient as you navigate through this process because my 7- principles for Exposing Your Hidden Self and Discovering Your Sparkle Effect will require self-reflection, trips back down memory lane, decisions making, some crying and purposeful pain. During this transformation some of the principles maybe difficult, don't let those difficult times frustrate you; it's just par for the course. When you feel like giving up just imagine yourself living life without the shadow (fear, limited beliefs, low self-worth, etc.). Keep your eye on the prize because you created on **PURPOSE** to live an authentic life with passion and power.

NOTE: If opening yourself to hurtful feelings cause you any emotional distress that you can't handle, please STOP reading and consult a professional.

I want you to know that I have personally applied each and every success principles that is described in this book. So, I know from firsthand experience that these principles work – and that they have the power to literally transform your life! Please don't misunderstand me. I don't claim to "know-it-all," Truly far from it. I consider myself like you, a "work-in-progress" and I continue to learn every day.

However, I know what it's like to believe that your life has no purpose, nor you have nothing to offer this world, because that's the kind of attitude I had for the more than half my life. I know what it's like to doubt yourself and your abilities, because again, been there done that. All of the positive changes that I've made in my life are the result of practicing the principles you'll read in this book.

As you move through this book, I hope these 7- principles are instrumental in your transformation to:

• become transparent with yourself

- expose the lies behind your limited self beliefs

- welcome more light and energy in your life

- make peace with your past, and

- allow the hidden you to be expose

- To discover your purpose and passions

Here's to your *SPARKLE effect!*

- Tawawn Lowe

Principle #1 - Accept, Believe and Know

Studies show that one of the things most people want to know is their purpose in life. A limited few know exactly what their purpose is, and they spend their lives embracing the journey to fulfill it, while the vast majority wrestle with questions such as "why am I here? What is my purpose? Does my life have meaning?? We all have asked these questions for different reasons. Most people ask because they desire clarity for setting specific intentions for their lives, while others ask because they have trouble believing that their lives have purpose.

For his song titled "1" (featuring Clipse and Posta Boy) Rapper Nelly penned the following lyrics: "I wasn't born on purpose; I was un-purposely born. I'm the result of what happens when the condom is torn."

Some may say these are just mere words to a song, and for them this might just be the case. But the truth is that every day, people show and grow up in the world and wander around aimlessly, believing that their lives lack meaning. They believe that there is no significance to their being because one or two negative acts, words, or circumstances have altered their reality and re-defined their perception of their lives.

Coming to the realization that your life has purpose may indeed be one of the hardest steps someone can take. When life has you in what feels like a vice grip, it's hard to see beyond the hurt, pain, and disappointment. Believe me, I understand. It's hard to believe your life has purpose when you were told you would never amount to much, or told you are just like your no good mother or father, or told you were good for nothing, or that you were stupid or ugly. Purpose may be hard to comprehend for a woman who longs to have children, yet has a barren womb. It's difficult to realize purpose when your life has more failures than successes, when life just keeps hurting, and you feel like there is no God.

When a person's sense of purpose is diminished, s/he can lose the capacity to believe. Then the questions come. Was I even born on purpose? What did God create me for? Am I good at anything? Am I good enough to be anything or anyone special? What do I have that my family or those around me even need? What are my gifts and talents? What is purpose and what is my purpose? The pondering can become obsessive!

Before you can answer any of those questions, you first have to accept, believe and know that you were born on purpose; that your life is no accident. The one question I can answer with certainty is that before the foundation of the world, God had a plan for your life and for mine. As a result, your very presence on earth is significant and inherently embedded with a specific mission designed for you and you alone. To believe that your life has no purpose or was an accident would mean that you believe God made a mistake when He created you. I have to tell you, that it is extremely unlikely and actually false to think that the Divine Creator of all life, Who thought to differentiate shades of green for grass – did not create you for a specific reason. Your purpose, I believe, grew in the womb with you.

God's plan for your future is for you to be exceptional, phenomenal and extraordinary. Does that mean that we will all become Oscar-winning actors, Nobel Prize winners or heads of state? Of course not!

If your life didn't have purpose, why would God give you life, gifts and talents within, along with all the other attributes that make you unique? He must have had some plan in mind with your name on it.

I must confess that I haven't always believed that I was born with purpose or that I always knew that there was something wonderfully special about me. I wish I could say that I always knew that there was value in my life. I cannot say any of those things. Like so many others, I spent a great deal of life just existing with no direction or purpose. Critical junctures in my life would raise those same but frightening questions "why am I here? What is my purpose?"

Because I didn't accept, believe or know that my life had purpose, I found myself stuck in a rut going nowhere fast for too long. I'm sure you're likely familiar with the pattern: we approach each day with the same routines preparing to get on our "hamster" wheels. Once we are on the wheel, we run and run and run, exerting lots of effort but going absolutely nowhere. Constantly do the same thing with the expectation that your life would magical without any action on your part.

The sting and stigma of Nelly's lyrics "I wasn't born on purpose - I was un-purposely born. I'm the result of what happens when the condom is torn," hit to the core of my spirit. I related not because of how I was conceived, but careless comments about my potential and destiny that had held me captive for a number of years.

When I was in the seventh grade, my teacher told me based on my low score on an aptitude test that I could not achieve as a professional beyond menial labor (specifically a cafeteria worker). *(PLEASE NOTE: This by no means demeans this line of work. If you are fulfilled and believe it is your life's calling is to serve in this way, then serve with pride and passion. However, I believe that this remark was made to me as a detrimental estimation of my potential and destiny.)* By adulthood, the words had replayed so much in my head that it had become my mantra. It was my justification when I wasn't accepted into the Marines (even though I was accepted in the Air Force); it was my rationale when I wasn't accepted by the first two colleges I applied to; it was vindication as to why I didn't get the jobs I desired, and it was my defense when all the business attempts failed.

The problem with these types of situations and declarations is they take on an energy that then creates incidents and cycles in our lives. Words of condemnation potentially create thoughts of condemnation which then become – you guessed it – acts of condemnation. Words like "You can't do that. You can't become that. You will never be good enough. You aren't unique. What makes you so special?" We hold these sentiments over our heads like umbrellas on rainy days and we stay hidden beneath them, even when the sun is fighting to shine just for you.

Limited expectations and negative words such as these become banners, and if we're not careful, they can end up becoming self-fulfilling prophecies. Words have power! Every day countless people show up in the offices of psychologists, psychiatrists, and clergy because they are reeling from words that deflected them from their purpose. Their quest for purpose leads them from here to there, because like me, they allowed someone else's limiting expectation over their life to become their reality.

Living life on purpose doesn't just happen for everyone automatically. There are some people who can live out their life's purpose as simply as they wake up in the morning. Their gifts and talents are often revealed and nurtured early in life, and they know that they are destined to be singers, athletes, actresses, politicians, or whatever they desire. Then there are the rest of us, who have to make the choice to find and live out our purpose. It's a process that requires you to look deep within yourself. The answers are there, like treasures, buried, and waiting to be discovered. Once you make that discovery and start walking that path your life changes.

It is upsetting when you feel like you've been walking through life without a true purpose. It impacts your self-esteem, your self-worth, and can cause you to be jealous of people who seem to know what they are meant to do with their lives. Living life without finding your purpose is not living; it's merely existing. But the truth is, with some introspection and digging, you can discover your purpose in life also. When you look at everything you have experienced in life, it is easy to imagine why you felt hopelessly lost. I challenge you today, look back over your life again, and choose to see that all of the experiences were about getting to your purpose, perfecting you for that purpose, and positioning you to reach it. Each change of direction in your life has made an important contribution to the person you are today. Your failures, obstacles, disappointments, negative sentiments, traumatic events are all about the same thing – getting you to your purpose and preparing you to live it out.

Living life on purpose is a choice. Each day we are faced with the decision to determine if we will live our best life and get the best life has to offers us. A purpose driven life is a commitment to live in the light and to allow your **SPARKLE** *effect* to change your life and the lives of others. It is up to you to take full responsibility for the direction you will take your life. Life is too precious to waste, and time is life. A life lived intentionally connected to your purpose and passion is far better than living without ever discovering your purpose.

ACCEPT ING YOUR MIND...

Adjusting your attitude concerning how you see, feel and think about yourself is vital to accepting, believing and knowing that you are commodity with something to offer that can change the lives of others, your community, and even the world. Accepting, believing and knowing that you are a person with purpose requires a shift in your mindset. Out with the old and in with the new thoughts about how you feel and think about YOU. Yes, I said FEEL because what you feel will dictate what you think, and what you think impacts what you accept, believe and know. Reprogramming your mind is essential to your destination. It is not an easy task, nor will it happen overnight.

Reprogramming your mind will start with the power of your own words to **SPEAK** your new truth. This is not a whisper to you; it is you saying it out loud so you can *hear* it. The relationship between conscious and subconscious is complicated, yet simple. Your subconscious mind has to repeatedly hear the new programming so it can be passed on to your conscious. You've got to tell yourself daily: I accept, believe and know..... The reason you have to keep saying this is because the more you say it, the more the words will take root, and you will start to feel what you are saying. How you feel is connected to what you think and believe. It's a little bit like forgiveness, you have to keep saying it to feel it and once you feel it, you can say it because you believe it.

When I started my journey of walking in my own shoes, changing my mindset was my biggest hurdle in my transformation. I had years of negative thoughts to remove, so I had to employ some drastic strategies. I will share a couple of these strategies and hopefully they can assist you in your transitions.

1. Mirror-Mirror Face-Time

Every day for 1 year, I looked in the mirror and told myself, "accept, believe and know." Each morning, and before I went to bed, I had what I called mirror-mirror face-time. The conversation went like this..."Mirror, mirror on the wall, tell me do you see what I see?" I would then reply to myself asking" What do you see?" Yes, I was talking aloud to myself, and NO I didn't feel crazy at all, LOL! My reply was the same whether I felt it or not, "YES, I see a woman who accepts, believes and knows she was born on purpose, with purpose, to live a purpose driven life."

The declaration was sealed with "AMEN" and a smile, so I knew I agreed with what I accepted and wanted to believe.

2. Scriptures and Affirmations

Every week I selected an affirmation and scripture that was charged with faith, power and conviction to speak life and power to those dead places in my belief system. I would repeat each affirmation and scripture several times each day, every day for the week, make them my screen savers, post them at my desk and on the refrigerator. The affirmations and scriptures had the same goal as the mirror-mirror face-time reprogramming the negative thoughts; and sending positive response to my subconscious.

3. Journaling

Journaling was a big part of my daily regime. I wrote every negative word I spoke and thought against myself. I wrote the circumstances surrounding my words and thoughts, my feelings at the time, and what is behind the negativity.

4. Prayer

I prayed for revelation and clarity of the things I exposed and God revealed. I prayed for strengthen for the journey.

The key is to accept, believe and know in your mind and heart that you were born on purpose. Once you know this – you will be ready to start your journey to finding your purpose.

Principle #2 - Expose the Hidden You

"You can't hide from yourself –
Everywhere you go - there you are."
"Teddy Pendergrass"

"Truth is the light, light shining within

when you look in the mirror do you see foe or a friend?

You can lie all you wanna but one day you're gonna,

gonna breakdown, breakdown and let it all out.

You see that you can't hide from yourself
everywhere you go there you are. I just gotta say,

that you can't hide from yourself everywhere you go there you are.

Make peace with yourself before you love another

understand who and what you are before you can go any further.

You can lie all you wanna but one day you're gonna, gonna breakdown, breakdown and let it all out.

You will see that, you can't hide from yourself

everywhere you go there you are. I just got to tell you, you can't hide from yourself everywhere you go there you are.

You can't hide, you can't hide

you look in the mirror- there you are. You walk down the street, well – look in the store window and there you go.

There you are. You can't hide, no. no, no. You might run, but you can't hide. You can't hide brother – you can't hide. You can't hide sister – you can't hide.

You can't hide no you can't hide. No matter where you go, well there you are. You can't run from yourself there you are.

You gotta deal with yourself. Sleep with yourself. You gotta be with yourself at all times. No matter what you do, no matter what you do, no matter what you do."

There was a time when these lyrics would send a flood of tears streaming down my face. To hear the voice of my conscience coming from the late, great R&B singer and funk preacher, Teddy Pendergrass was a painful reminder that I was falsely representing myself to the world, my family, and my friends. I felt like Teddy alone knew my secret -- that I had spent more than half of my life as an impostor. I had willingly joined the ranks of millions who live by mainstream society rules that you never show weakness or vulnerability.

At an early age, I discovered that pretending to be somebody I wasn't was a great defense mechanism to help me navigate through my insecurities, protecting and enabling me to survive in this big bad world. I didn't want to expose the yuckiness of my wounds because it would mean that everybody would be able to see the depth of my pain, anger and despair. Like most people hiding behind a mask, I didn't want others to know I had high level of self-doubt, overwhelming feelings of inadequacy, and a deep lack of confidence.

For a very long time, only three people (God, me, and Teddy Pendergrass ☺) knew how that statement made by my seventh grade teacher, haunted me from my teens to my mid-30s. I regret to say that I carried her words like a badge of honor, turning them into a self-fulfilling prophecy. This was my excuse for all my disappointments, failures and shortcomings with everything I attempted to accomplish.

To escape the insecurities, feelings of inadequacy, self-doubt inflicted by my 'secret', I created a mask that didn't allow me to care much or feel deeply about much of anything or anyone.

Then, I added another layer to the mask so I could fit in, because I'd started to notice that most people really couldn't handle the extra sting I added to my already strong personality. I had learned early that my mouth was a weapon, and I used my weapon as part of a disguise. The world teaches us to mask (hide) everything, your family secrets, domestic violence, and sometimes your faith. What it doesn't tell you that years of wearing the mask will warp your sense of self.

On some level we are all facing a common fear – we are afraid of being seen for who we believe ourselves to be. We are afraid of confronting our limiting beliefs and we avoid facing that fear by hiding. People have a universal fear of exposure; whether physical or mental. We cringe at the thought of feeling naked or unsafe. Hiding behind a mask mitigates the risk of exposure and if we are exposed, less frightening. So we add layers of "stuff" and accessories to the whole costume that masquerades as credibility.

Removing the mask and coming out of costume isn't an easy task, it takes time, energy, self-reflection and commitment. You can do this, and I know this because I have. Here are a few things that helped me with removing my mask:

- Realize that your mask is not who you are. Acknowledge the fact that you created this mask, this act, as a defense mechanism for your survival, that it was valuable and had a use temporarily, but it is no longer required.

- Identify and list what lies beneath the mask(s). This list will likely contain some fear of failure (or success), insecurity, low self-esteem, feelings of inadequacy, and lack of self-worth.

- Determine if you are hiding based on your own outlook and limited belief or someone else's predictions for your life.

- Look for situations and patterns in your life that caused you to wear a mask. These situations would have encouraged you to conform in a manner that was pleasing to someone else, or step into someone else's shoes.

- Use the power of visualization and see yourself literally shedding the mask. See the life you want to create that is aligned with your purpose, passion and power. Replace the vision of impossibilities with possibilities and keep your focus on letting the world see the authentic – real YOU!

- Be aware of the costs and limitations that wearing the mask has created in your personal and professional life.

- Be committed to do doing whatever it takes to reintroduce yourself to your authentic self. Your goal is to stop hiding and discover your *SPARKLE effect*.

Okay, here comes the really hard part that accompanies removing the mask.... Think for a moment, when was the last time you told someone "

I'm sorry, will you forgive me because I forgive you?"… Now when was the last time you said those words to yourself?

Naming, claiming and shredding the mask(s) only shift you slightly from behind the shadow - your next step is to release the negativity.

When you unmask and begin the journey towards authenticity, it becomes important to release yourself from the things you have done to yourself. In order to stop hiding behind yourself and expose the hidden you, you will have to make peace with your past, and yourself. You must be willing to forgive yourself for the things you have done to yourself. This is this important because if you can find forgiveness in your heart for those who have caused you hurt, you should be able to apply that same forgiveness to yourself.

Unforgiveness is a place of darkness where the overcast of confusion hides light and energy. Your *SPARKLE* **effect** can only illuminate when you are willing to forgive yourself. Self-forgiveness is a key element in practicing healthy self-care and self-love. When you can forgive yourself, you give yourself permission to let go of part of yourself, the part that wants to keep you full of regret and entangled in guilt, shame, fear, and resentment.

Many of us are hard on ourselves. We punish ourselves for the bad choices and mistakes that we made, but self-forgiveness must be an option for your emotional and spiritual well-being. Self-forgiveness is the gift you owe yourself and that you deserve. It is a method to relieve you of regret and condemnation, while allowing you to acknowledge that you made some mistakes. Simply put, it provides you the opportunity to heal, and make peace with your past.

Self-forgiveness is a gradual process that may take time. It starts with valuing yourself and making a resolution to stop letting the past continue to haunt the present. It is an intentional re-direction of the person you are now to re-route you to your purpose. Self-forgiveness is what we do for ourselves to enable us to become whole and move forward. It should be a regular part of your physical, mental and spiritual self-care regime.

Earlier we talked about going into the darkness of your mind and heart to identify those things that keep you hidden behind a mask. Now that you have identified why you wear the mask, it is time to let go of the hurt and pain to acquire closure. You have to go to that dark place -- the cemetery in your mind and heart to close those unfilled graves that serve as gaping wounds on your soul. This is probably the hardest part of any person's journey through life -- to face-off with one's self to ultimately make peace with one's self and one's past. It is not enough to identify your internal 'open' graves. Once you have identified them, you have to be willing to accept responsibility for anything that you have done to yourself. You must be ready to commit your shame, guilt, regrets, and hurts to the ground. Visualize yourself laying each hurt to rest. Go into as much detail as you feel necessary. Use this prayer to help you with forgiving yourself…

Dear Heavenly Father,

"I understand that there is nothing to gain by holding myself in unforgiveness and there is everything to gain by releasing myself from unforgiveness and beginning the process of healing. I want to move forward, and let go of those things that separate me from You and Your will for my life. Because Jesus died for my sins, I choose to forgive myself. I will no longer be angry or punish myself. I forgive myself for letting this hurt control me, and for hurting others out of my hurt. I repent of this behavior. I ask for Your forgiveness and healing. God help me to never again retain un-forgiveness of myself or others. Thank You for loving me, and for Your grace to move forward with You."

Your final words to be spoken over the filled grave are "I'm sorry, I apologize and I forgive me."

Keep living your life one wonderful day at a time. Be conscious of any masks you may be wearing and look for opportunities to shed them. Being true to yourself can take time, especially if you are not used to doing so. Celebrate your success and recognize that you are doing the best you can and living a life that is true to who you are at the core.

Be confident in who and what you are; don't hide it! Uncover your vision and purpose, then live them. I know that it is easier said than done, but it's time to get out your own way, stop playing the blame game, and start the life you deserve.

Stop hiding behind yourself! Remember, baby steps are great and can lead to huge rewards. Unmask! Share the great talents that you were given for all to see. I have no doubt that you are an amazing person! When you remove the mask, you give the world the opportunity to see all that you are and have to offer. Be free to give yourself the gift of authenticity -- being yourself. Remember, the same forgiveness that you extend to others was designed for you as well.

Here's to unmasking and self-forgiveness!

SELF-REFLECTION QUESTIONS:

1. The most important thing that you can do right now is finding out what is limiting you. What are some things that are keeping you from achieving your dreams and goals RIGHT NOW? Identify them, so that you can eliminate them. (Examples: lack of money, procrastination, self-sabotage, feeling helpless, not enough support of family and friends, etc.)

_____

_____

_____

_____

_____

_____

2. The first step to taking off your mask is realizing that you have one on. Are there any times that you act less than genuine? Does this happen in certain social circles? When do you feel uninhibited and completely free to be yourself?

_____

www.tawawnlowe.com

_____

_____

_____

_____

_____

3. Are there people around you who are not giving you the support you need? Does it feel like any time you try to accomplish something, they don't have your back? Talk to these people, see why they are this way, and assess whether or not that relationship is positively-charged or part of you "walking in other's shoes".

_____

_____

_____

_____

_____

_____

4. Who are the people in your life that have repeatedly been there for you? Take time out of your day to thank them in your own way. It may seem like a small, silly gesture, but I guarantee it will make someone's day. Let them know that you are there for them too; this builds a mutual support system.

_____

_____

_____

_____

_____

_____

I bare my nakedness to the world that the world may see who I am, not the mask that hides my flaws, not the mask that hides my beauty. "I am blessed this moment, I am embraced, I surrender only to love." "Let nothing frighten you whatsoever. You are a child of eternity." Never ever give up. There is no goal too difficult for those who believe in their destiny. Heaven is so much nearer than we often think it to be.

Principle #3 – Start the Journey

NEW BEGINNING

You have made the major choice to begin a new chapter in your life. This includes smaller decisions such as: being more positive, intentionally unmasking to find your authentic self, and reaching your full potential. You have made the choice to find your purpose in life. It sounds pretty big, doesn't it? Well, don't get worried or overwhelmed. The following chapters are going to tell you everything you need to know, and will hopefully be the guide you need to be successful in this new venture. This is an exciting time!

First of all, and this is very important, let yourself feel GOOD. You are making a change. You are changing your life. You are getting out of your own way and are going to feel and do and see things you never let yourself feel and do or see before. This is a time to feel proud, to enjoy and love yourself for doing something good for you. As you will find out, doing something good for others starts here. And since we are all called to do for others as we would wish to be done to us, then you can rest assured that you're on the right track.

Positive reinforcement is critical. This process of self-discovery is not going to happen overnight. You need to feel confident to be able to pick yourself up on those bad days, shake off any negativity, and stay on the path. Your journey is a long one, but be comforted by the fact that the only one stopping you is you. YOU are in complete control, no one else. This is your game, your turf, and YOU CAN WIN.

In a society where we have been conditioned to expect things instantaneously, we are quick to be displeased and discouraged when things don't immediately go our way. This is going to be one of your toughest obstacles. As we discussed in earlier chapters, it's going to take TIME. It's been said that time heals all wounds and it certainly changes perspective. Things that seem cataclysmically awful at one moment -- when reexamined and re-analyzed -- may be not be as awfully unbearable as we once thought.. Patience is key, and overall, patience with yourself is most important.

DON'T THROW IN THE TOWEL

How many times have you experienced a series of events that had you sitting alone with your head in your hands and asking aloud "Why me?" Sometimes, life throws things at you so hard and so fast that it makes your head spin, and it's all you can do to just stay afloat. You can get lost in a tailspin of despair and find yourself at the bottom of a well where your fears are free to prey on you.

This happens. Life happens. But the important thing to remember is that when all these things pile up and seem to overwhelm you, it is a TEST. It is a test of your will, resolve, and faith. And in order to get out of this well, you can start off by being comforted by the fact that you're not alone. Everyone has been there and in fact many live most of their lives in the well. Your goal is to find the strength to climb out of it and then hopefully, help others to do the same.

There are positive and negative energies in the universe, and sometimes it's just your turn to spend time in negative energy. This often feels like everything is working against you, like nothing is going your way, and that the end is nowhere in sight. It makes you feel helpless and hopeless. It is days like this that make it feel impossible to take off your mask, even though it is so important that you do, because the mask is like a security blanket in that it gives you a sense of protection. It's almost as though you believe that if you can pretend hard enough, and convince others that nothing is wrong, and then there will really be nothing wrong. It seems like backwards logic when you spell it out, but I can guarantee you that we do it all the time. It's a survival technique. But the point of life is not to just survive; it is to live.

The solution to that feeling of "why me" is very simple. Time and faith. As I said earlier, it's been said that time heals all wounds. I know that some days it's possible to forget that the bad things that are happening are only temporary.

FAITH WITHOUT LIMITS

What is faith without limits? It is not questioning whether or not things can be done and just doing them. When you only question and do not act, the answers will not manifest. When you sit and cry and mope and feel sorry for yourself (and yes, I know this sounds harsh. It's tough love, believe me ☺) you will never be able to break the cycle to take off the mask. Believe in yourself, have faith, and make sure that that your faith is limitless. (This should apply to every aspect of your life.)

One of the reasons I'm so adamant about this is because it's innate to me. (It's one of God's personal gifts to me.) Having faith without limits comes naturally to me. But this may not be the case with all people, and it certainly wasn't the case with me before I started the journey of living a purpose filled life. I resisted. I questioned. Only after I sincerely opened myself to it, and chose to accept that I was capable of having limitless faith, was I able to truly wield it like the powerful weapon it is.

If you find yourself in that dark place where you see no light, and you're asking yourself "why me?" then I say to you to be patient; take a deep breath, and know that it takes time to come out of that place. It takes you being open to and ready for change. If you are ready and willing to embrace change, it will come. It always does. And then the power of positive energy kicks in...

Think about it. Negative energy is attracted to negative energy, just as positive energy is attracted to positive. So when negative things happen and you only focus on those negative things, there is a higher possibility that more negative energy will be drawn to you. Think of someone you know who is generally happy and carefree. The main reason people can be so light-hearted is because they focus on the positive. Yes, life is hard. Yes, bad things do happen. You can't have the positive without the negative; that's how it is for everyone. But it is your choice whether you want to spend your time being positive or negative force in this life.

FOR A GREATER PURPOSE

There is a reason why all of this -- the work to be accepting-believing and knowing, the stripping off of the mask(s), forgiving of yourself, etc. -- is so important. It goes back to being created for a reason.

Everyone is born with a purpose, and inherent in all of us is a longing to do good, to connect with others and to lend a helping hand. In order to help others, you must help yourself. You must be a positive force, showing others by example how they can better their lives and improve their outlook. When you find your passion, as we will highlight in the epilogue, you will know exactly what tools you have been given to do this universe good. You will know in your heart that you can do anything.

As you are in the process of removing your mask and shedding the layers of untruth to walk your true path, there will be things, ugly things, that rear their heads to try to break you back down. They will try to make you take cover and hide once again. If you see this start to happen, don't get discouraged. And if you slip, remember the key is self-forgiveness.

Sometimes traumatic things from the past rear up to hinder your future progress. All the things that made you hide and pretend to be someone you're not can resurface. It may be something that happened to you, some injustice or cruelty that was outside of your control, like a tragedy. It may be something you did that was embarrassing, or perhaps an act of naiveté that spurred negative consequences. Regardless of what occurred in the past choose to recognize it for what it is; now is your chance to address those memories and move forward.

When this happens, and the fear returns, it is time to forgive. Forgive yourself for those things that you did or said. Forgive those others who caused you pain. Holding on to these things is only making you miserable. And yes, the world is full of things that are unfair, but remember that it is your CHOICE to be happy. Let go, forgive completely. You will find yourself feeling that a weight has been lifted and that you feel cleaner and clearer if you have truly accepted the past, forgiven and let go. THIS is a huge challenge, a huge step towards a new life. You have broken down a huge wall that has been keeping you from being your true self, from being truly happy!

When momentous strides like this are made, it's important (and even essential) to reward yourself and to let yourself feel good. I promise you it will also encourage and inspire you to do more good. Every step you take, from the baby ones to the long strides, speeds you up on your journey like a snowball rolling down a hill. You will feel lighter, laugh and breathe easier, and be ready for new challenges with more confidence, less fear.

YOU GOT THIS!

It is not going to be easy, but it is 100% doable. It's all about having the patience to weather the time it's going to take, and having the faith in God and in yourself to keep you going. Remind yourself that you were born with a purpose, that your true self is a beautiful thing that should never be covered, and that you can do anything.

You have to believe in yourself. If you believe it, you can do it. Yes, it takes time to get to that point. When you've been afraid of something for most of your life, the residue will linger and stay with you for a time. But every day, every single day that you walk on this earth with the focus and determination to rid yourself of that fear, you will shed it with every move you make. Look at time as your ally and companion on this journey.

Just like forgiveness between people can take some time, self-forgiveness can too. It's not always automatic. You have to be aware of your feelings, work to accept them, and then summon the courage to forgive and let it go completely so it can never hinder you again.

Just remember that when a relapse happens (and it may) all you need to do is: (1). Recognize it and (2) Don't let it in the door. KICK IT OUT ON ITS BUTT! This is YOUR show! YOU run this! You are in control, baby! You've come this far, and in the next chapter we will talk about the power of words: the power to harm, to heal, and most importantly to empower.

SELF-REFLECTION QUESTIONS

At the beginning of this chapter, I asked you to let yourself feel good. This may sound silly, but it really is important. I mean, that's the whole point of this, right?? To feel great! SO...

1. What are some situations that you experience on a daily basis that get you feeling down, angry, upset, etc.? (e.g., long lines at the bank; running late to work; being unhappy about your weight/body issues, and so on...)

_____

_____

_____

_____

_____

_____

2. What are some things you can do short term (quick fixes) that will be able to get you back on track to thinking positively?

_____

_____

_____

_____

_____

_____

3. What are some long-term things that you can do to solve those problems? (e.g., work out more; wake up earlier, etc.)

_____

_____

_____

_____

_____

_____

4. How strong is your commitment to do those long-term things? You need to figure out if they are

doable. There is no point in making promises you can't keep. Make a plan, and start with something manageable that you know you can work with and go from there. (Example: If you're always late and that frustrates you, and you'd like to start waking up two hours earlier, it may be a good idea to start smaller, say, with 30 minutes. Once you accomplish that and feel good about it, you'll have the motivation to do an hour, an hour and a half, and then eventually two hours!)

_____

_____

_____

_____

_____

_____

"There are two mistakes one can make on along the road to truth... not going all the way and not starting."

Buddha

"I believe that life is a journey, often difficult and sometimes incredibly cruel, but we are well equipped for it if only we tap into our talents and gifts and allow them to blossom."

Les Brown

"The first step towards getting somewhere is to decide that you are not going to stay where you are."

Anonymous

"It may be that when we no longer know what to do, we have come to our real work, and that when we no longer know which way to go, we have begun our real journey."

Endell Berry

"No one else can speak the words on your lips. Drench yourself in words unspoken. Live your life with arms wide open. Today is where your book begins. The rest is still unwritten."

Natasha Bedingfield

Principle #4 - Understand the Power of Words

Our vulnerability to words is intense. From the time we are conceived, unless there is a physiological challenge, we are conditioned to respond to spoken words. Expectant mothers are encouraged to speak to their unborn children. There is energy, a transference of power and emotions that come through words. That is also why many in the medical field, encourage loved ones to speak to patients who are in a comatose state.

All humans crave affection, the warm regard of others, love, friendship, etc. We form our relationships through communication. Relationships may end because of a lack of communication. There is a connection in words. Every word that passes from person to person is weighted, and thus that weight hits us at different impacts. The weight may be jolting. The weight may be lifting or it may be stirring. Every word absorbed – primarily spoken – but also written and read, has power to do something. What are your words doing in your life? What are your words giving to those around you? Are your words aligned with your values and purpose?

We have all heard the adage, "sticks and stone can break my bones but words will never hurt me." As children, some of our parents used these words to try and teach us a lesson about not letting what people say negatively about us adversely impact us. The concept that words will never hurt us is a lie from the pit of HELL. If this was true, there wouldn't be so many commercials for anti-depressants. Fifty percent of what causes most of us harm is not what was done, but what was said. Don't get me wrong; sticks and the stones can break your bones. But words...

Our words have power. The power of the spoken word (or words) is one of the things that distinguish human beings from the rest of the animal kingdom. While it's obviously true that animals communicate, humans are the only species who have developed spoken communication which can be translated into beautiful poetry or moving speeches. We have also learned to harness the power of words to hurt, heal, and empower.

I have no doubt that you have experienced the power of words first-hand. The sting of someone verbal assault against you, the relief of comforting words, the regret of saying something you wish you could take back, are evidence that words potent. It's an unfortunate truth, but people's words can hurt you intentionally or accidentally, and leave scars. Each time the memory surfaces from one of those injuries, you may find yourself angry, ashamed, and bitter.

The most important thing about realizing that all words have power behind them, is also realizing that YOU can choose the words you speak and the words you choose to ingest. When my 7th grade teacher told me I would never be more than a cafeteria worker, who would have known that I would carry those words in my spirit for more than half my life believing her limitations for my life.

When you are haunted by words that demean, criticize, judge you, or make you feel ashamed you need to focus on letting in the words that speak life, the positive words, and banishing negative and hurtful words from our life. What does this mean? It means the next time someone talks down to you, or tries to break you down with words, do not accept those words into your psyche or your soul. Do not let them affect you. Consequently, this also means that the next time you lose yourself in rage or anger, you do not throw negative words at others. Remember that negative energy brings on more negative energy.

A GIFT YOU CAN KEEP...

There is a story about Buddha (that I will paraphrase here) that teaches a wonderful lesson. The story is about a man who is upset with the Buddha's teachings, which he sees as a bad influence on youth. He is so angry in fact, that he decides to find him, and kill him. This man approaches where Buddha is sitting, and starts aggressively recounting all the reasons he believes he is bad. He informs Buddha that he hates him, and his purpose for being there is to kill him. Buddha stops him before he gets too close by calmly asking a simple question:

"Are you a very important man?" Buddha asked.

The man responded, "Why yes, of course I am. I am very important!"

Buddha continued, "And since you are an important man, do you often entertain guests in your house?"

Puzzled, the man says, "Well, of course, from time to time I have other important people in my house. Why do you ask this?"

"And..." Buddha continued in his questioning. "...these people who visit you, do they sometimes bring you gifts?"

"Yes, sometimes they do. Why?" The man was now more baffled than before.

"And what do you do," asks the Buddha, "If you do not like the gifts they bring you?"

"Why, I refuse them. I tell them to keep them." The man replied. "But what does this have to do with anything?"

"You coming here is like that. You bring me this negativity, this yelling, these threats, and I do not like them. I do not want them. Keep them for yourself."

The man's jaws dropped!

"And..." continued the Buddha "My teachings are the same for you. I only want to help; but if you do not like my teachings, you do not have to accept them. You may refuse them, just like I may refuse your negativity."

You get the final say in whether or not something someone said is going to hurt you, or is going to help you. If you like the words that are offered, if you appreciate what they have said, accept it graciously, and spread the positive energy. If you do not like it, if it is hurtful or insulting, *then that is a gift they can keep.*

This is what I mean when I say you choose. It is entirely up to you. You get the final say in whether something someone said is going to take root in your psyche and your soul and cause you harm, or if is going to assist in increasing the quality of your life. If the words are like a honeycomb to your spirit, accept the words graciously, and spread the positive energy. If you do not like it, if it is hurtful or insulting, then that is a gift the bearer can keep.

EMPOWER YOURSELF...

You are the only one who gets to decide who has power over your happiness. There is only one person you should let have power over your happiness. Here's a hint: It should only be you!

Accept the good, leave out the bad. The good words will nourish you like honey, and make your words sweeter and sweeter so you can spread that positivity to whomever you speak to, always paying it forward.

Steel yourself against the bad, do not let it enter. Shrug it off like an old coat and swat it away like it's a pesky fly. In this way, you give good words power. Ignore anything that threatens to break you, and by doing so, empower yourself.

I will tell you, it's not always easy. Our vulnerability for the impact of words is so strong, it's set into us from the time we are babies. Other's opinions and impressions of us makes us vulnerable to hurtful words and eager and desperate for praise. It is that dependence, on making people like us, that makes us helpless to defend ourselves when those cruel words come.

Do not be helpless, be strong. It's not easy sometimes to shrug off words that are designed to attack us, to hurt us. It is not always obvious that the motive behind the words is to hurt us. Just keep in mind that you are a being of positive energy now. Remember that you will only accept that which makes you feel good and makes you feel empowered. It takes practice and it takes you being actively aware of the words YOU choose to use.

Again, the more pleasant and kind your words are, the more likely you will be to receive pleasant and kind words from others. It is very important that you actively practice this.

PICK YOUR FRIENDS LIKE YOU PICK YOUR FRUIT...

The goal is to accept the kind words and banish the negative words. This is important with both incoming and outgoing words. If you're trying to control what you say and what others say to you to get the maximum positive energy, just think how this is impacted by the people around you. If you surround yourself with people who are constantly putting you down, who are not supportive, and who lead you to negative tendencies, then your task of focusing on the positive becomes a lot harder, doesn't it? Whereas, if the people around you are happy, are good and loving family and friends that support you and want happiness for you, then this makes the struggle much less difficult.

Choose the company you keep wisely. As you progress on your journey, in order to stay on the path, you will need support from time to time. The people around you play a supporting role on your journey. If there are those who would hinder you, who would pull you back or knock you off track, there is absolutely no reason to let them do so. You can choose to release them to let allow them to walk their own path. Be sure to choose the people who support and love you for your *true self* -- *t*he "you" without a mask.

What I'm about to share next, may seem a little callous, but it's necessary. There may be persons in your life who you don't want to release. You may even think that they have your best interest at heart when they try to dissuade you by telling you to "get your head out of the clouds" or that you must "stay grounded in reality." What you need to (lovingly) share with hem is that you prefer and are equipped to make those decisions on your own. At times like this, it's imperative that you tell them that while you appreciate their concern, you are in a position to decide and determine what's best for you. You and only you decide what you can and cannot dream and what you can or cannot do.

BREAK THE CHAIN, BREAK THE SELF-FULFILLING PROPHECY...

One of the most important things about perfecting the art of choosing which words you let have power over you is being able to address negative words that you internalized. These are the words that have gnawed at you when spoken; or have been replaying in your mind – secretly haunting you.

Perfecting this skill will unleash a new world or power that is rightfully yours. You are going to reclaim that power that was taken from you. It is the power to let yourself be free, and break the chains that have been holding you back.

This is a great step on the journey and it is necessary if you are going to stop hiding, unmask, and become the best you that you can be. You must realize that the words that hang over you are yours to control, to do with as you will. For me, it was the limiting words of my teacher stopping me every time I tried to reach a goal beyond being a cafeteria worker.

Cutting, cruel words of the past can end up becoming self-fulfilling prophecies. But now that you know the power of words and the power you have to choose, you can reject those words and find strength in defying them. Be strong in your resolve, and keep your mind and heart open to the truth, open to the positive flow of energy. Work to intentionally to banish negative thoughts and feelings that cause you to have a low self-esteem and imagine about yourself. Love yourself, and surround yourself with people who really love you. Choose your words carefully, and be independent enough that you do not let other's negative words hurt you or bring you down. Know that your words have power, and that other people's words only have the power that you let them have. Choose positivity every time. This way, you will be empowered with every word, and you will be taking bigger and bigger strides on your journey to being your best self; and creating a life you deserve.

SELF-REFLECTION QUESTIONS

1. List instances where you have undoubtedly felt the power of words. Try to come up with 5 times where someone's words affected you with negative energy.

_____

_____

_____

_____

_____

Now, try to come up with 5 times that someone's words have affected you with positive energy.

_____

_____

_____

_____

_____

2. Do you believe your words have power? Think of times when your words have affected others, positively or negatively.

_____

_____

_____

_____

_____

3. The next opportunity you get, use your words and spread your positive energy by saying something kind or uplifting to someone. This could be a stranger, a friend, or a loved one. Feel that positive energy flow back to you. Repeat this exercise at least 3 times daily, even when (and especially when) you're not feeling too happy. I guarantee it will make you feel better! Write what you might say below.

_____

_____

_____

www.tawawnlowe.com

_____

_____

_____

4. Think of a past or future scenario where someone says or has said negative things to you. With your new knowledge and awareness, how would you now turn the situation around and have them keep that gift?

_____

_____

_____

_____

_____

_____

QUOTES ON FRIENDS AND THE POWER OF WORDS

"Only hang around people that are positive and make you feel good. Anybody who doesn't make you feel good, kick them to the curb and the earlier you start in your life the better. The minute anybody makes you feel weird and non-included or not supported, you know, either beat it or tell them to beat it."

Amy Poehler

"A friend is one who knows you and loves you just the same."

Elbert Hubbard

"Handle them carefully, for words have more power than atom bombs."

Pearl Strachan

"Words are the keys to the heart."

Chinese Proverb

"If someone were to pay you 10 cents for every kind word you ever spoke and collect from you 5 cents for every unkind word, would you be rich or poor?"

Anonymous

www.tawawnlowe.com

"Confidence in the goodness of another is good proof of one's own goodness."

Michel de Montaigne

Principle #5 - Adjust Your Attitude

Every single day is a gift. Every single day that you wake up, and are still on the path, you should feel rejuvenated and excited for what new things the day will bring.

As you continue your journey, as you deal with the issues of life and work to forgive things that happened in the past, always strive to find the positive energy in everything. Every single day that you do this crucial work you will be rewarded by a tomorrow that is sweeter and easier to handle.

Every time life throws something to you, it will be easier to catch, and easier to deal with without feeling lost or helpless. You will know what to expect from yourself, and you will have the tools and the strength you need to overcome any obstacles. Every time you overcome something, you are made that much stronger, and that much more prepared for life's next speed bump.

We all can agree that a bad attitude generally leads to negative results. If your attitude requires some a "positivity" adjustment, you can easily do it depending on your beliefs and actions. Changing your negative traits can be achieved through positive thinking and hard work. How will you know that your attitude has changed? The answer lies with your thoughts and feelings. If you think and react and respond positively, you WILL change.

By now, you have probably realized (and prayerfully begun) to embrace the fact that we will come to several crossroads as we move through this journey called life. How we process the crossroad and make decisions at them is based solely on our attitude. I know you heard the saying, "attitude is everything." Life is sweeter and more manageable when we approach it with a progressive, healthy and positive attitude.

NEW ATTITUDE

My focus in this chapter is to give you an idea of the ideal attitude to have. What do I mean by attitude? I'm referring to the viewpoint from which you look at life, the feedback you give to yourself to others and to life itself. This determines how things affect you, how you let them affect you, and how you affect others around you.

Everyone comes to a crossroads in life. In fact, there is never just one, there are many. By reading this book and seeking to become the best you can be, and starting to live your life on purpose and create the life you desire, you are taking on a new attitude.

With every new choice come new challenges. The challenge of having a completely new mindset seems daunting at first, but if you have already started doing the exercises and working on yourself as discussed in previous chapters, then good news -- you are already on your way!

The integral part of this new attitude, in fact its driving force, is going to be positive energy. Strive to be a light bulb, constantly shining with the positive energy and outlook you've built up from believing in you, forgiving yourself, changing your self-talk, and not accepting negative energy from others. This is not always easy, but I guarantee it is the happiest possible way of living. Developing a positive lifestyle and attitude is a choice. This has been one of the key factors in my transformation; and how I have become who I am today.

That doesn't mean that there aren't hard days. There are days when I slip back into that dark place and when my light "goes out"... but that is when I draw from my well of support. I draw from God, from true friends and family. There is always light around you, if you open your eyes to see it. You can use it and draw from the love and strength around you to relight your inner you. You will never fail, if you keep this in mind. Nothing is ever as bad as it seems.

MAKE A CHANGE...

As you continue to work on yourself, you may find there's still something that's not right, that there is still something holding you back. It may be a job, a person, or a situation. Whatever it is, it just seems to be constantly tugging on you, dragging you back to the darkness, keeping you from spreading your wings. If something is not fulfilling you for whatever reason, don't accept a defeated attitude. No matter what keep an attitude that says: I CAN DO ALL THINGS!

There is no reason for you to settle for less than you deserve. You deserve everything, and if something is keeping you from achieving total and complete happiness, kick it out of your life! No excuses! No ifs, ands or buts!

There have been countless times I let things get in the way of my happiness and success -- namely, fear. There were times I wanted to look for a new job because the job I had was not fulfilling, but I was so scared about what would happen if I left that I forfeited a lot of opportunities. I was consumed with fear when in reality, I always stood a good chance at getting a better job. Over the past several years I have started several businesses, but I never believed they would succeed and thus, they crumbled. If I had really believed in myself and what I was doing and let my actions manifest my beliefs; i.e., done everything I needed to in order to make the businesses successful, I'd be rich! But instead I was my own greatest hindrance because I was afraid of succeeding; afraid of what it would mean, afraid that it would be "too hard". So I never finished my races or I'd always caused myself to come in last place.

There are many opportunities that we miss because of our negative attitudes. These attitudes present themselves as anger, procrastination, slothfulness, indecision and in my case -- fear. This is why it is so important to build the strength -- the faith in yourself -- to make decisions confidently. Sometimes these will be difficult decisions to make such as moving to a new town, starting a new page in life, releasing someone who doesn't want the best for you, quitting your job, etc. Sometimes decisions such as these are hard to make, but they are necessary if you want to move forward, if you want that better life for yourself.

How can you adjust your attitude? You can use the following tips as your guide:

Assess yourself: Do you think you have the right attitude? Hint: If your self talk sounds a lot like "Poor me; my life isn't what I want it to be", or "None of this is working and it's not my fault" or "Nothing ever works", or "maybe it's just not meant to be", your attitude is on the wrong track. But the good news is you can challenge yourself to develop an attitude that does not resemble defeat.

Explore what you're feeling: If it's mostly positive, nourish that, grow it, and keep the momentum going! If it's negative, why are you feeling that way? If you're saying "poor me" where is that coming from? What is making you sad? Why are you feeling like you'd rather throw a pity party than fix the problem? Is it because you think you don't know how?

Identify the negative things, the bad things in your life that are holding you back from being the most positive person you can be. Is it a person, situation, job, mindset, or your own self-esteem? Whatever it may be, acknowledge it, name it, and then work to *change it.* Only YOU can change your attitude, and you will LOVE the way it feels once you've made that change. Embrace your freedom, embrace your choice.

SHARE IT...

You can pay the positivity forward. Refrain from negativity (directed to yourself and towards others.) When you reach a place in your life where you are comfortable with who you are. Have found your purpose and passion, it's time to share your gifts with the world. As a person of light on this new path to making your life better, there is only one way to keep up the trend, to keep the positive energy flowing, to keep everyday as fresh and bright and wonderful as possible. The only logical step is to do everything you can to make the world around you a better place. I'm not talking about saving the world, being a superhero, or even running for office; (although, if that is what you are called to do then you definitely should do it!) All I'm saying is to give of yourself. I've learned to do it and you can too. I actually got to a point where I just couldn't contain it. I realized my gifts, and recognized myself as a person with power, the power to spread positivity and be a help to everyone around me. Once you change your attitude you should gain a different perspective of how you see view yourself and the world. Your new outlook helps you interpret and respond to challenges differently. This is what attitude adjustment is all about.

It's a NEW DAY, and as you strive to get out your own way to let your *SPARKLE effect* shine, being able to adjust your attitude is key. One of the most important steps you can take towards achieving your greatest potential in life is to learn to monitor your attitude and its impact on your life.

1. What is the most "negative" time in your day? Is it when you arrive at work? When the alarm clock goes off? Driving in traffic? Think of some ways that you can inject positive energy into that time, to make it easier to get through and keeps the positive energy flowing!

_____

_____

_____

_____

_____

2. There are going to be times when your great mood and attitude will be tested, by anger, annoyance, sadness, etc. What are some things that you know make you almost instantaneously happy? Is it pictures of your pets or loved ones? Is it funny jokes? Find ways to make these things easily accessible to you to create rainbows on those dark days.

_____

_____

_____

_____

_____

_____

3. Make a call list or set speed dial settings for the positive people in your life, the ones who always seem to cheer you up. Let them know that you have chosen to put them on that list to call when you are unhappy for any reason, because they always seem to turn your frown upside-down.

_____

_____

_____

_____

_____

_____

4. At the end of every day, before you go to bed, write down 3 things that you learned, or that were new to you, or that made you laugh, or that you really liked about that day. That way you go to bed thinking about the good things, and that will make you excited about the new day ahead!

_____

_____

_____

_____

_____

5. A good rule: Do one good deed a day! The best thing about paying it forward is that it always comes back around, sometimes unexpectedly and when you need it the most.

_____

_____

_____

_____

POSITIVE ATTITUDE QUOTES

It is very important to generate a good attitude, a good heart, as much as possible. From this, happiness in both the short term and the long term for both yourself and others will come.

Dalia Lama

If you don't like something, change it. If you can't change it, change your attitude.

Maya Angelou

Choosing to be positive and having a grateful attitude is going to determine how you're going to live your life.

Joel Olsten

Your living is determined not so much by what life brings to you as by the attitude you bring to life; not so much by what happens to you as by the way your mind looks at what happens.

Khalil Gibran

Principle #6 – Have Faith without Limits

"Jesus said unto him, 'If you can believe, all things are possible to he who believes.'"

Mark 9:23

I mentioned faith without limits in earlier chapters. Now I want to dedicate this chapter to explaining exactly what it means, what it did (and still does) for me, and what it can do for you. God gave me this phrase in 2007, and I have been standing on it ever since, believing that everything will come together and that the pieces will fall into place for me. This is going to be one of your ultimate tools.

"Hatred stirs up strife: but love covers all sins"

Proverbs 10:12

There will be times – times that you may already be experiencing- when no matter what you do or what you tell yourself, you will feel like you just don't have it in you to keep going. Try as you might to get up or to reach higher, life just seems to keep pushing you back down. These are the days when you feel like God just don't know your name.

In this difficult journey to live a life of purpose, the thing that you will need most is strength. The strength to stay positive, the strength to love when there is so much hate, the strength to endure, and the strength to have faith when life seems hopeless. This is the hardest task in building a new life. This is the uphill battle that you must fight in order to stay on the path and to keep improving yourself.

I will tell you how to win that battle and how to find that strength. It is the only way I know how, because this is what enabled me to survive through everything, and come out of it better, stronger, and happier than ever.

FAITH WITHOUT LIMITS.

Have limitless faith in all areas of your life and allow God to be control of your life. When what you need is strength, put all the strength that you have into your faith, and it will return to you tenfold. That is the truth of faith without limits.

This is no easy journey. When I felt cornered, depressed, and like I had nowhere else to turn I turned to God. In reality, my problems are so small in the grand scheme of things. Who better to remind me of that? Who better to calm and soothe my troubled mind, to gently pull me back to sanity and peace than the one who created us all?

We are created in God's image but we are far from perfect. What better reminder of what love is, of what good there is in the world, than the unconditional love the Father has for us? Despite the hatred and evil, despite all of our everyday sins, feeling meek, and tired, and broken down, He has infinite strength and infinite love.

Draw from Him. Draw from the never ending well of strength, the never ending well of love, and find that you can get through whatever you're facing. You can make it to the next day, through the next hardship. Realize that there is more than just bad luck, down days and hard knocks ahead. There is love, and success, and positivity all around you. Your faith should serve as a constant reminder of that.

You can also learn to draw on the love and strength of others, the ones around you who love you unconditionally. These are the people who will be your biggest supporters, your greatest allies, the springs and fountains of love and comfort. Draw on them. Let them be your well in addition to your faith. This is going to be the source of your strength -

your light in dark times. When all the hate and hurt in the world threatens to swallow you whole, picture their faces, and hear their words; you will not be alone.

This is the greatest lesson that I learned. Having faith without limits, having a sanctuary, a place to recover, will enable you to draw strength, love and support from it. This is how I was able to overcome and so will you.

"And he shall be like a tree planted by the rivers of water, that brings forth his fruit in his season;"

Psalms 1:3

So, since you've made it to **Principle #6**, you've been reading, understanding, and maybe even starting to implement the changes in your life on this new path. You may have made huge strides, you may have made baby steps, but either way you are succeeding.

That is the ultimate goal: helping yourself to succeed. Doing everything you can to give yourself the life and the happiness that you deserve. Being completely and 100% true to yourself is no simple task, but neither is just getting up and out of bed in the morning on some days! The whole point of all of this work and focus is to build up your strength.

You are building the strength you need to be whoever it is that YOU are, your true self, without hiding from anything or anyone. Building the strength to get through those rough days when life slaps you hard in the face, and still be able to say, "Okay, so it's going to be one of those days, but I can do this." With time, you will be able to just shrug it off! You are building the strength to not dwell on the past, to not let yourself be swallowed by grief, or by thoughts of the life you used to lead. You are building the strength, not only for yourself, but for those around you and be a positive influence for the people in your life, to be a role model.

But when you feel completely empty, beaten, void of all the knowledge and love and positive energy you possess, this is when you draw on God. Draw on His strength, by remembering your faith. Believe and know that all of these bad things that happen, every single one of them are a TEST. He is testing you, testing your resolve, and testing your strength. Just as any parent must let their children test the waters, attempt to support themselves on their own, and tentatively flutter from the nest, so to speak, He is also letting us see how we do unassisted.

It is in this way that we grow, grow strong, and blossom into the person we always wanted to be. For me, who I've always wanted to be (and who I finally became) was a confident, capable woman who could do anything she set her mind to. You are growing. You grow by going through every day with a focus on positive energy, by drawing from your well of strength when things get bad, and enduring, for the sole purpose of being able to reap the fruits of your labor. And then you taste the sweet nectar of freedom when you realize that you did it, you have changed. Your life is not what it was, and when those bad days come around and try to knock you down again, you will say "No. I've tasted my freedom. I've got my well of strength. You can't touch me."

"As the whirlwind passes, so is the wicked no more; but the righteous is an everlasting foundation."

Proverbs 11:25

Do you know what the best part is? The changes don't stop. The time when you recognize that you have indeed made a difference in your life, when your eyes are opened to that wonderful realization, that is only the beginning. Every time you experience a success, a new one is forming! It will snowball and keep going as long as you have your well of strength and love, have limitless faith in God, your family and friends, and yourself.

You have so much more in store, so much more ahead of you. And soon, you can use all of this newfound positive energy, all of this new strength and wisdom, and begin to apply it to the world around you. You can share your gifts with others, and in doing so, receive infinitely more in return.

SELF-REFLECTION QUESTIONS

1. Think of a time you lost your faith, or felt like you were going to lose your faith. What would you do in that situation now?

_____

_____

_____

_____

_____

_____

2. Think of a time when your faith came back to you, or grew stronger because of an event or action. What was that event or action? Could you use that experience to strengthen your faith again?

_____

_____

_____

_____

_____

_____

3. Think of a time when you felt like God was speaking directly to you. What did it feel like? Would you be open and able to hear Him speaking to you now?

_____

_____

_____

_____

_____

_____

4. You are more than likely someone else's support and a source of strength and love for them. What do you actively do to help them when things get hard? These are things that you should not be afraid to ask of them when the time comes for you to need support.

_____

_____

_____

_____

_____

_____

5. Open your eyes to everyday experiences in life
that renew your faith in God, that renew your faith
in family and friends, or renew your faith in
humanity. Keep a record of these. They are the
things you must not forget; you will need them to
remind you of good on the bad days.

_____

_____

_____

_____

_____

_____

FAITH QUOTES

"A faith is a necessity to a man. Woe to him who believes in nothing."

Victor Hugo

"A man of courage is also full of faith."

Marcus Tullius Cicero

"As your faith is strengthened you will find that there is no longer the need to have a sense of control, that things will flow as they will, and that you will flow with them, to your great delight and benefit."

Emmanuel Teney

"You block your dream when you allow your fear to grow bigger than your faith."

Mary Manin Morissey

"Every tomorrow has two handles. We can take hold of it with the handle of anxiety or the handle of faith."

Henry Ward Beacher

"God didn't promise days without pain, laughter without sorrow, or sun without rain, but He did promise strength for the day, comfort for the tears, and light for the way. If God brings you to it, He will bring you through it."

Unknown

"Keep your dreams alive. Understand to achieve anything requires faith and belief in yourself, vision, hard work, determination. Remember, all things are possible for those who believe."

Gail Devers

Principle #7 - Be Your Own Cheerleader

On your journey there will be times when you will have to stand alone in your pursuit of happiness. It will be in those moments when you will need to be your own cheerleader. The only person you will be able to count on is you, and when you need that word of inspiration you have to be willing to give it to yourself. This is not to say your support system won't be there. But the reality is that they can only carry you so far. This journey is yours and you have got to have that GO GET 'EM attitude when other people can't do it for you.

Being your own cheerleader means you often maybe required you to say you GO to yourself, motivate yourself with your own self-talk, and keep the positive thoughts and energy moving.

Remember, you are 100% responsible for your life. Your motivation is not contingent upon other people, but your attitude about yourself and your success. When you transfer this responsibility to other people you often time set yourself up for disappointment.

The following are some things that I know of that kept me going, they always have and always will. In this final chapter I just want to send you on your way with some reminders, advice, suggestions, and well-wishes.

AVOID THE NEGATIVE

When things do get hard, remind yourself to stay away from the negative. It's a perilous and slippery slope, and if you take one step down that path, you run the risk of reverting back to where you started.

You know how there are times when you're down, feeling bad about yourself, and no matter what anyone else says it doesn't make anything better? Well, those are the times where you have to be your own cheerleader. No one else can do it for you; it has to come from within.

Instead of getting down on yourself about something that didn't work out, focus on the positive, focus on what you *did* get done. It really is that easy! When you set foot on the positive side, other positive things will greet you. Every good thing that has happened comes to light, everything that you feel grateful for, and everything that you are looking forward to will appear and set you straight. Just like that you can be back on your path.

Always bear in mind the universal rule that negativity brings about more negative energy and positivity brings more positive. Since it's hardest to be positive when things aren't going your way, if you actually do manage to come out of it, you will be stronger for it. How many times have you heard the phrase "What doesn't kill you makes you stronger"? It's true. Be a fighter!

LAUGH

Laughter makes you feel better; it's even been scientifically proven to make you healthier! Laughter is the universal medicine, and if you don't believe in its power then you've never let it heal you. Laugh easily and laugh often, because as the saying goes "laugh and the world laughs with you; cry and you cry alone."

Be sure to let light and laughter into your life at all times. It's one of the measurements of positive energy, and if you're still not sold on the fact that positive energy attracts more positive energy, then the next time you see someone laughing in a room, and those around them begin to laugh in turn, know that it's working.

I'm not trying to suggest that you run out and purchase a book of jokes (unless you feel so inclined.) What I am saying is you should let yourself feel lighter and easier about everything. Let yourself have a jovial disposition. When you do, the down days will happen less often and feel less impactful.

Keep in mind that situations that make you feel happier and laugh more often are generally good signs that you are in the right place. People, friends, places etc., can be judged if they are right for you or not depending on your light-heartedness. Use laughter as your compass, and it should never steer you wrong. Then when things seem to get really tough, give yourself a healthy dose of laughter.

LOVE

Open yourself up to love fully and completely. Love deeply. Don't limit yourself to romantic love, although romance is a beautiful thing when found. What I mean is to radiate love -- love for yourself, love for your family, love for your friends, and love for all human kind.

If we are made in God's image and Jesus is God's only begotten son, as God's children, what we have in common is a duty to love all just as Jesus taught. Unconditional love is hard to come by, and harder still to do/give unconditionally, but it is achievable. If it is God's will for us to do it, then it's part of our purpose in life, just like finding your passion.

For a lot of people, this is not something that comes easily, as we are conditioned to be wary of others. I'm not suggesting that you should not be cautious of others who may mean you harm, but I am recommending that you try to open yourself up, and let yourself love a little easier.

This is especially important when it comes to loving *yourself*. Self-love is one of the most important loves of all. Yet for some reason it is often the hardest to achieve. At times it's easy not to like yourself, or put yourself down or focus on your flaw rather than celebrate yourself. When you are able to look in the mirror and look deep inside to your true self and *love* what you see there, then you will know that you can truly be happy.

Work on loving who you are. It is only when you love yourself that you can truly love others. I promise, the better you make your life, the easier it will be to spread the love. And as the Beatles put it "And in the end, the love you take is equal to the love you make."

LIVE

We were put on this earth for a reason. We have all been a precious and beautiful miracle in the gift of life. It cannot be taken for granted and we must give it absolutely everything we have. It must be lived, and *really* lived, to its fullest potential. Life is too precious to be wasted.

This is your charge. This is your task. Live your life. *Live your life*. I realize that this sounds simple, and at certain times it is, but then there are other times it just won't seem that easy. There's so much strife, so much hardship, so many, many challenges to endure. But it's my firm belief that we are all born with purpose and we are all meant to be happy.

So we must overcome our struggles and grow. Every day we must grow wiser, stronger, and hopefully happier than the day before. We are seeds that should be allowed to grow to their full potential as God and life intended.

If you think about it, we already have the upper hand! As human beings, we are given the *gift* of truly being able to appreciate all that this life has to offer. The greatest gift is love – it is the one gift you must not let go to waste.

If you agree, I ask you to really give yourself the chance to live life to the fullest. To LOVE yourself and give yourself a chance at the life you deserve, the life you've always wanted. I know that it is possible; I have faith in you, and I wish you every happiness!

SELF-REFLECTION QUESTIONS

1. Think back to when you were a child about your favorite activities and list them. Which of these tell you more about yourself? Which ones made you feel the best? What do you think you can do today that would give you the same feeling?

_____

_____

_____

_____

_____

2. If you know people who seem to be living their dream life, ask them how they did it, how they made the choices that brought them to this great life and list them below. Learn from others, always ask questions, and start the discussion among friends and family that benefit you and support you in living life to the fullest.

_____

_____

_____

_____

_____

_____

3.   What are some of the goals you have set for
yourself now? (Short and long term.)

_____

_____

_____

_____

_____

_____

4. If you don't have any goals now, why not?

_____

_____

_____

_____

_____

_____

5. Do you set goals for every aspect of your life? Why or why not?

_____

_____

_____

_____

_____

_____

PASSION AND GOAL SETTING QUOTES

"The great and glorious masterpiece of man is to know how to live to purpose."

Michel de Montaigne

"Nothing great in the world has been accomplished without passion."

Georg Wilhelm Friedrich Hegel

"If there is no passion in your life, then have you really lived? Find your passion, whatever it may be. Become it, and let it become you and you will find great things happen FOR you, TO you and BECAUSE of you."

T. Alan Armstrong

"A strong passion for any object will ensure success, for the desire of the end will point out the means."

William Hazlitt

"The significance of a man is not in what he attains but in what he longs to attain."

Kahlil Gibran

"The ability to convert ideas to things is the secret to outward success."

Henry Ward Beecher

"Unless commitment is made, there are only promises and hopes; but no plans."

Peter F. Drucker

Epilogue...

This is it. This is the time and the moment you been waiting for since reading Principle #1. It's time to know and acknowledge that you were born on purpose. Now that you know your life has purpose, it's time to find that which God has created you for. It's time to find your purpose.

Don't let this scare you. This is the awakening every person desires – finding their purpose. This is the chapter of your life that will change your life forever. I know it feels crazy because you don't know, but it's not the end of the world. Heck, most people just don't know either! Now that you're on the right path, the next step is to find that thing that you were made to do.

It may not be one thing; it may be several. I personally believe that whatever your purpose is, one of the best ways to recognize will be the way it makes you feel. I believe when you tap into your purpose you will know it intrinsically and intuitively. Your purpose is likely whatever makes you feel that you are your *true self.*

This is why it is so important to live life without that mask. If you're wearing the mask, how do you know what's you, who you really are, what you really like, or want? How are you going to find your true purpose if you're not being your true self?

OBSERVE

If you are one of the many who doesn't readily recognize your passion or your true purpose, your first step should be self-observation. Look inside and ask yourself some deep questions and give yourself true answers. Remember, this is time for real truth talk, no lies with yourself -- especially since lies aren't going to help you find YOUR truth. What do I mean by lies? Well, if you're asking yourself "What do I *love* to do? What makes me feel truly like myself?" the answer is absolutely not going to be "playing video games". It's not going to be "drinking and partying". It's not going to be "going shopping". These are superficial and are likely part of your mask. Dig deeper and be real with yourself.

When I say dig deeper I mean: you like video games, but that's not the reason you were created. What is underneath that? Problem solving? Enjoying the art of the game? The design of the game? The action in the game? Find out what's underneath the surface, and take it from there.

If you think your true purpose is "drinking" or "partying" you're not truly on the right track. What's underneath that? Party planning? Making connections with people? Bring people together with common interests? Uplifting those around you? Get down to what it is you really, really like about it.

Shopping can be fun, but you need to look at what's behind the shopping before you identify it as a passion. What about fashion? Interior design? Art? Taking care of others? Buying things for other people to show you care? The challenge of finding a great deal? What is it about shopping that makes you feel happy?

LOOK BACK

Anyone could tell you one or more things that they used to *love* to do as a child. In fact most children, if you ask them, know exactly what they want to be when they grow up. Ask people you know what those things were that they wanted to be, think about their answers and ask them what changed?

Look back into your past – after all, your past is what made you who you are. Now that you're taking your life into your own hands, look back to the innocent parts of your past. Look to the positives to give you direction. What fascinated you as a child? What did you long to do above all else?

As children, most of us are not taught that we have a purpose, that we were born for a reason and that we must look for it. Now you are in a place where you are being your true self, you are living for yourself and for others as a positive being. Now, as an adult, you must learn of and teach yourself the passions you had as a child.

When I was very young I decided that I wanted to be a missionary. I just felt like I knew that was what I was meant to do. Later on, as a teenager and young adult, I decided that I wanted to be a child psychologist. I didn't do either of those things in the end, but looking back, I see now that the common thread is helping others. That is my purpose.

GENERAL TERMS

When you are looking for your passion, try to be as general as possible. Don't limit yourself to one specific profession in one precise area. Instead, I encourage you to think about everything in broad terms. The whole point of finding your passion is to *un-limit* yourself. Rid yourself of the limitations that others have placed on you as well as the limits you have ever put on yourself. This is the thought you should go on: If you had only a year left to live, what would you want to be doing?

Here are some examples of general areas of interest to look for:

Active – how active you enjoy being, how busy you like to keep yourself.

Social – how much you enjoy meeting people, talking to people, and making connections.

Creative – how big your creative streak is, if you have a love for any kind of art or creative process.

As you determine and refine your interests, you're likely to see what you were made do to. Again, everyone is born for a reason and with a purpose. Just as we started as seeds, there are seeds inside of us, the seeds of our purpose (our God-given purpose), that we need to find and help to nourish and grow.

When the seeds of our purpose grow, we find our passion. When we fulfill our purpose by embracing and implementing our passion, we plant the seeds of happiness and positivity in others.

It is my firm belief that the reason we were born and given the miracle that is our lives is solely to spread love, light and happiness into the world by fulfilling our purpose. God gives us life. God purposely created you so that you could have a chance to fulfill your purpose.

By finding your passion, by living a life of light and positivity, you will not only be your happiest, but you will spread that happiness to others because you are doing what you *truly love*. You are doing what you were made to do. If that's not the whole point of life, I don't want to know what is!

GET TO KNOW YOURSELF

This journey, as you well know by now, takes a lot of introspection. This is a beautiful thing. Get to know yourself.   Get to love yourself.   Find confidence. Discover the things that make you, *you*. By acting on your passions, on things that you love, you are celebrating yourself. Everyone should live life this way.

Life is fleeting. This is why I cannot stress enough how important it is to live it to its fullest extent. It is critical to be your true self, to follow your true purpose, and live life without limits. As far as we know, you only get this one chance... one chance to live, love and laugh to your utmost potential.

You have a beautiful soul. You have a beautiful mind. You are unique in every way. *USE* everything you've got, *DO* everything you can, *LOVE* every bit of yourself in this life. You may not find your passion immediately, but don't despair. As long as you are living life to the fullest, doing the things that bring you happiness, and being true to yourself as a being of light and positivity, your passion is bound to find you.

READY, SET, GOALS!

Now that we have some direction by searching for your passion, it's time to get down to business! This is the time to set goals and start making your dreams, and your perfect life, a reality. It's not going to be easy though, so make sure you're ready to be your own spin coach! You may have lists of things that you want to do, business ideas, potential jobs, or new interests and hobbies that you'd like to explore because they make you feel good. All of this is fantastic, and you're going to be very excited, so just be sure to keep that energy up!

Before you dive in though, you need to get organized. Clean house, literally and figuratively. Make sure that you have a clean slate in your house, and in your life. If there are things that you don't need, in simple terms, you need to kick 'em to the curb. Disassociate yourself from persons who are not positive influences. Quit bad habits. Implement good ones and get ready for this new phase in your life. Do whatever you need to do to feel fresh and ready to set goals for yourself and work for the life you've always wanted, the life you deserve!

What tools will you need? Do you need to make phone calls to find out about opportunities (jobs, going back to school etc.)? Do your research and make sure that you know what you're getting into, no matter what it is. Get yourself prepared.

Another important thing to do is to let supportive friends and family know what you're planning. . Talk to them about your interests and your plans so they can be prepared to support and help you. You will be surprised how fast people will jump out of their seats to help! Here's another thing to think about: People are attracted like magnets to people with big ideas, who are trying to make their lives better, who are really, really *living* their life. They see it and they want it for themselves, they want to be a part of it; it's infectious!

USE YOUR IMAGINATION - SEE THE VISION...

Sometimes it seems like nobody dreams anymore. When did this happen? People just tell you what you need to do and you do it. That's not the way. Children are encouraged to use their imagination, but somehow as we mature, we lose this along the way. This got me wondering....why don't adults get to imagine? Instead we become entrenched in our gray, day-to-day and don't let ourselves dream. I'm here to tell you that you must dream in order to be happy.

Visualize everything that you want: happiness, fulfillment, luxury car, job, spouse, the bank account statement, the children, the beach house, the ministry, business, degree(s), the healthy body, clear mind, and spirit that loves God. Imagine what you want for yourself. Go into as much detail as necessary because this is going to make it real for you. If you can see it, you can achieve it. This sounds corny, but it's so true. How can you work for a better life if you don't know what that life you want looks like?

It's okay to daydream, because your new task is to manifest those dreams into realities. While you're looking for your passion, and even once you've found it, keep dreaming. This is going to sound silly, but set aside 10 to 30 minutes each and every day to let your mind wander, to let your imagination run away with you. This will ensure that you stay on the right path. There have been studies that show that people who daydream have better ideas, are happier, and are more successful. Not only are you getting ideas for your real life by seeing what your dreams are.

While you are planning and setting your goals, make sure you let yourself dream. This is going to hold you to your end destination, and the whole reason you started this journey: to live a happier and better life.

MAKE YOUR PLAN(S)...

It always helps me to carry around 1 to 2 notebooks so that I can write down all of my ideas, all of my plans, and sketch out my future. This is so very important. It is essential to plan because people can dream all day but what gets things done is planning. Dreams must be followed by planning. With today's technology, your smartphone or tablet can give you the same option.

Make sure you have a do-able strategy, keep it realistic. This doesn't mean limit yourself, but it's just not good to bite off more than you can chew, that's almost a sure-fire way to get overwhelmed, which puts you in danger of giving up. Be sure to ask your support group, friends and family for help. You will be surprised at their willingness to assist, and it will also help you manage big tasks if you have more than one person on your team.

One of the most important things to do once you have created your plan is TO STICK TO IT! Life will hold unanticipated challenges which will modify the game; that's a given, instead of resisting it, anticipate it. Hold yourself to your plan but adjust it if/as necessary. This so often is where others are thrown off course. Don't let this happen to you.

If it helps, have other people in on the plan who can remind you of your goals and hold you accountable. Have a workspace that is a sanctuary so you will look forward to getting work done, or doing the things you need to do to get that dream job, to find that dream home, to do whatever it is that you want to do. Notebooks, calendars, and planner books are going to become your best friends.

SET YOUR GOALS...

Your goals are going to serve as your map. How will you reach your desired destination if you can't see where you're going? These are going to be your guiding lights, the structure and foundation of all of your plans. These will help hold you accountable to your dreams.

Remember the notebook, cellphone, the planner and the calendar? You used them to lay out your plan, and now you're going to use them to set your goals. These are the tools with which you will build you dream life. Fill your calendar with deadlines and due dates, all of the things that are going to determine how your plan is progressing. These can possibly be subject to change, because as we all know, life happens. Just be sure that you don't extend indefinitely!

Your planner should be full to the brim with meetings and the everyday actions that will need to be completed in order to get things done. This is going to be a little overwhelming at times, but hey, no pain no gain. You're on your way so know that your hard work will always pay off in the end. Fill your trusty notebook with ideas, notes, thoughts, and the fruits of your research. If you have an iPad or computer that can serve as your notebook too, just make sure that it is available to you 24 hours a day, 7 days a week, because you never know when you'll need it; inspiration strikes at all sorts of different times!

ENERGIZE YOURSELF...

Pump yourself up! You've got all these new ideas, all these things that you want to try, that you want to learn, that you want to do. This is going to take some serious *work!* So you need to be sure that you keep your energy up, keep your goals coming, keep smashing the deadlines you set for yourself! It's going to seem overwhelming at times, but you know what? You can do this!

You may not be Superman or Wonder Woman, but you are capable, smart, and strong and you are equipped with the force of positive energy on your side. Keep your eye on the prize, work hard, stay faithful to your goals, and before you know it, you're going to be at your destination, and happier than you knew you could be.

You are ready to live life on purpose.

Here's to your success!